Goodrich Castle

Jeremy Ashbee

Introduction

Standing in open countryside above the River Wye, Goodrich Castle is one of the finest and best preserved of all English medieval castles. Despite its setting near the Anglo-Welsh border, the castle led a largely peaceful existence, and its ruined state is the result of a single violent episode during the Civil War of the 17th century.

A castle has stood in this area since the 11th century and the site still contains a small keep built in the 12th century, probably by Richard 'Strongbow' de Clare (d. 1176), who achieved fame as conqueror of Ireland in the 1170s. The castle's defences were upgraded when it passed to William Marshal (d. 1219), one of the greatest soldiers of his time. But Goodrich was largely rebuilt in the late 13th century after Henry III gave it to his half-brother, William de Valence (d. 1296), an influential figure at the royal court who accompanied Edward I on crusade in 1270. At Goodrich he created one of the most up-to-date castles of its period – an impressive defensive shell, concealing residential buildings of extraordinary complexity and architectural sophistication.

The castle survived, slightly altered in the later Middle Ages, until 1646, when its Royalist garrison was forced to surrender to Parliamentarians after a two-month siege, and much of the castle was ruined by mortar fire. In the 18th and 19th centuries the overgrown ruins became a magnet for visitors in search of the Picturesque or attracted by the castle's historic associations.

Above: The giant Goliath depicted as a fearsome knight, from a mid-12th-century manuscript. At this date Goodrich Castle was owned by Richard 'Strongbow' de Clare, one of the most renowned knights of his day

Facing page: The south curtain wall and ditch of the castle, looking towards the south-west tower

The Tour

Though the first stone castle with its tall keep dates from the 12th century, it was largely rebuilt in the late 13th century by William de Valence. He created a complex baronial palace within an outer shell of concentric curtain walls and massive round towers.

FOLLOWING THE TOUR

The tour starts at the castle barbican and gatehouse and follows a suggested route around the castle's residential buildings before exploring the outer defences and ditch. The numbers beside the headings highlight key points on the tour and correspond with the small numbered plans in the margins.

THE APPROACH

The modern approach to Goodrich Castle follows – at least in its final parts – the route by which visitors arrived in the late 13th century, when the castle was newly rebuilt. From the first sight of the castle at the end of the lane, the red sandstone south-east tower dominates the view. As you draw closer, the tallest feature, the slender 12th-century keep, appears to the left of the tower, its greenish stone contrasting with the other towers and curtain walls. The path turns east, then north, to skirt the edge of a deep cutting in the rock. Visitors here were not only in range of bowmen on the battlements, but were also confronted with a series of architecturally commanding features.

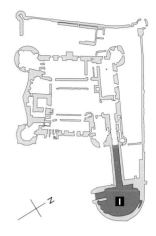

▮ BARBICAN

The path ends at the first of the castle's buildings, a fortified enclosure or barbican in front of the gatehouse, where visitors would be greeted and probably dismount from their horses. Like the barbican at the Tower of London, begun in 1275 for King Edward I (reigned 1272–1307), it has a semicircular courtyard and entrances at right angles, joining the barbican to the surrounding land by a drawbridge and to the castle by a stone causeway. This similarity may be more than imitation: Edward I sent royal workmen to Goodrich in 1296 while his uncle, William de Valence (d. 1296), was serving him overseas.

The barbican originally contained a small gatehouse and guard chamber facing the approach. Only the lower parts of the walls remain, with stone benches around the walls, perhaps sheltered by a pentice, or lean-to, roof. In the thickness of the north wall is a latrine chute. A narrow ramped stairway at the barbican's north-west corner beside the causeway formerly led down into the outer ward.

Below: Reconstruction of the Tower of London's Lion Tower, which was probably the model for the D-shaped barbican at Goodrich
Bottom: Goodrich Castle looking west, with the barbican in the foreground
Facing page: The gatehouse and causeway

CUTAWAY RECONSTRUCTION OF THE GATEHOUSE IN THE 15TH CENTURY

1 Drawbridge

2 Fighting platform

3 Gates

4 Portcullises

5 Murder holes

6 Guardroom

7 Latrine

8 Soldiers' room (possible)

2 GATEHOUSE

From the barbican, a stone causeway leads up to the entrance to the castle, the formidable main gatehouse. Though it has lost its battlements and the upper fighting platform that once projected from the towers, it still gives an excellent impression of its former strength and how it was used.

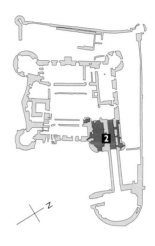

The 13th century had seen great advances in the design of castle gatehouses, with ever more complex combinations of drawbridges, portcullises and 'murder holes' (for dropping projectiles from above). However, in several of the finest examples – such as Harlech, Caernarfon and Caerphilly in Wales and Tonbridge, Kent – gatehouses also contained rooms on their upper floors for living and for religious worship. The builders of Goodrich were clearly aware of these trends.

The gatehouse at Goodrich is remarkable and in some ways unique. From outside, its most obvious feature is the asymmetry of the round towers flanking the entrance. The much larger tower on the left was built with a chapel occupying its ground floor. The large window here, recently restored, was inserted in the 15th century to light the high altar, replacing an even taller 13th-century window. Though numerous castles contained chapels directly over doors or gates, a location beside the entrance is unusual. The corresponding turret to the right contained only a guard chamber, and as a result could be much smaller.

The gate-passage presented visitors with a daunting sequence of defences, traces of which survive in the stonework. First was a wooden drawbridge, now replaced by a fixed bridge which fills the roadway in front of the gate. The original bridge pivoted beneath the gateway, with three swinging counterweights to tip the bridge upwards. On the left-hand side of the roadway are the stubs of arches that held a stone fighting platform, from which soldiers could shoot down on attackers below.

The gate-passage itself could be closed by two pairs of wooden gates, of which the holes for the wooden drawbars can still be seen in the side walls. The passage was further strengthened by two portcullises – now marked by vertical grooves in the walls – which were lowered by winches in a room above the gateway (see page 12). Still more protection was provided by murder holes in the vault, and thin windows or arrowloops in the side walls, from which archers could shoot into the passageway from the rooms to either side.

Halfway along the gate-passage, a door on the right leads into a narrow vaulted passage built into the thickness of the wall. To the right, the passage ends in a rectangular guardroom, which is covered with a rib vault and was heated by a hooded fireplace; slit windows allowed the guards to watch for new arrivals. To the left, the passage leads to a small latrine for the sentries.

Below: The remains of the gatehouse and its approach causeway

Accommodating the Noble Household

Goodrich Castle was built for the large and complex household of a great 13th-century nobleman, William de Valence. Identifying who lived where is a challenge for the modern historian

Many of the rooms around the courtyard and in the towers contain fireplaces, window seats, washbasins and latrines, signs that they were meant to be inhabited. Even this extensive accommodation, however, would have been inadequate for the full household of up to 200 people, not counting visitors: probably only the most important people lived inside the castle, with others lodging outside. Reconstructing who stayed in each room involves examining the ruins, translating the medieval documents, comparison with other sites and ultimately guesswork.

At many medieval castles, the most important rooms would lie beyond the end of the great hall, furthest from the kitchen. This would be the north-west tower and north range at Goodrich, which almost certainly contained the chambers and 'solar' of William de Valence and Countess Joan. More fine rooms for family members and guests lie on two floors of the south-east tower and the top floor of the south-west tower. Other buildings, including the east range, the rooms over the gatehouse and perhaps the keep, were probably used by household officers, soldiers and servants. In the late Middle Ages, upper floors were added to the east and north ranges, creating more rooms. The household was probably no larger than before, but its members now enjoyed greater privacy.

1 Great hall (possibly accommodation for servants)

2 North-west tower (lord's and lady's chambers)

3 North range (solar or great chamber)

4 Gatehouse (accommodation for soldiers, chaplains or the constable of Goodrich)

5 East range (accommodation for servants and officers, with cellars and latrines)

6 South-east tower (accommodation for household and guests on ground and upper floors)

7 Keep (possibly accommodation for servants)

8 South-west tower (very grand 'guest' room on top floor)

3 COURTYARD

Once through the gate-passage, you emerge at the north-east corner of the central courtyard of the castle, a good point from which to appreciate the castle's layout. The courtyard has always been dominated by the tall keep in the centre of the southern side, ahead of you. The keep is the oldest surviving building at Goodrich, dating from the mid-12th century. Almost all the other buildings around the courtyard were rebuilt in the late 13th century for William de Valence. To the right of the keep, along the west side of the courtyard, is the great hall, which survives in good condition, though roofless. The horizontal moulding, or string course, midway up its wall and the stone kerb around the path in front show that there was formerly a covered walkway running along this side and possibly all round the courtyard; in the later Middle Ages, this area may have resembled the cloister of a monastery. In the north-west corner of the courtyard (to your right) was the castle well, rediscovered during clearance of the ruins in the 1920s. It is 51m (168 ft) deep.

The ranges of buildings to the east (left) and north (right) are much more fragmentary. Fortunately, the people they accommodated are much better known. We know from the financial accounts for the year 1296–7 of William de Valence's widow, Joan, countess of Pembroke (d. 1307), that on occasion the castle would have had to accommodate nearly 200 people. Where they were all housed is a matter for some debate (see feature opposite).

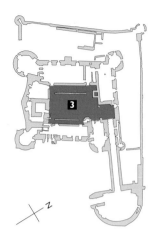

Below: The east range, south-east tower and keep, seen from the courtyard

Above: The west face of the gatehouse. The closed upper door to the left of the large window gave access to the chapel from the lord's apartments, probably built in the 15th century but now demolished
Below: An artist's impression of the interior of the chapel as remodelled in the 15th century

GATEHOUSE WEST FACE

Turn to look back at the gatehouse. The rear face of the building shows changes to this part of the castle, particularly the scar of an adjoining roof (midway up the small window on the left), and an upper doorway to the left of the large window. These traces indicate that in the late Middle Ages (probably the 15th century) there was another building here, linking the gatehouse directly to the castle's north range. The upper floor of this building (whose level is shown by the stone corbels in the curtain wall to the left) cut across the head of the earlier gatehouse arch, while a walkway at the same level, overlooking the courtyard, allowed the lord and his family to pass directly from their chambers in the north range via the high-level doorway into a raised gallery or closet at the west end of the chapel. The servants entered the chapel by the door at ground level.

4 CHAPEL

Go through the door into the chapel. The chapel occupies the southern half of the gatehouse, including the large semicircular turret which contains the apse for the stone altar. It was first constructed in the late 13th century and, though it stood without a roof (or a floor) from 1648 until the late 1950s, several features of the original building survive. To the right of the altar are a trefoil-headed sedile (the niche containing the

priest's seat) and a piscina (a sink for washing the holy vessels used in the Mass), and to the left is an aumbry (a cupboard for the sacred vessels). The household accounts of Joan de Valence mention at least nine chaplains or clerks, most of whom would have travelled with her household, performing administrative duties besides singing Mass and other offices; in 1296, the household was also joined by a party of preaching friars. If some of the better documented contemporary royal chapels are anything to go by, kneelers and praying-desks would have been provided for the heads of the household, leaving the other household members to stand behind.

As at several other castle chapels in the 13th century, the proximity to the entrance gate affected the design. To the left of the altar is a slit window, pointing into the gate-passage; and still closer to the altar is a socket in the wall which would once have held the drawbar for one of the castle's main gates. All three window embrasures contain stone window seats like those in the castle's other chambers. In the Middle Ages, the chapel was not solely used for religious purposes: a document of 1297 mentions that oats were kept in it, and the cellar below (reached from the building on the south side) is more likely to have been a storeroom than a crypt.

The chapel underwent a major reordering, probably in the 15th century, when a timber upper balcony was inserted at the north-west corner. This could be entered at first-floor level from the buildings, now lost, to the west, but a stone stair in the thickness of the north wall, cut through the back of a window seat in the side of the embrasure, allowed the lord to descend to the main floor level on feast days. The east end of the balcony was supported by a wooden beam spanning the width of the chapel. This rested on the stone corbels carved with angels bearing shields that can be seen in the side walls. Immediately beside the corbels are two further piscinae: these suggest that two more altars were added at the west end of the chapel in the 15th century, perhaps for the devotions of lower-ranking members of the household.

The modern stained-glass window at the east end was designed by Nicola Hopwood and installed in May 2000: its central motif represents the meandering course of the Wye.

The glass in the large 15th-century west window was unveiled in June 1992 and commemorates the personnel of the Radar Research Squadron who lost their lives during the development of Radar. On 7 June 1942 a fuel leak caused RAF Halifax V9977 to catch fire and crash, 1.5km (1 mile) south of Goodrich Castle. All 11 on board were killed, among them the pioneering engineer Alan Blumlein (1903–42), who had worked for EMI on what later became stereo sound and television. The plane was flying a test mission for the prototype H2S Radar system, which was designed to identify ground targets at night or under heavy cloud and later employed in bombing raids.

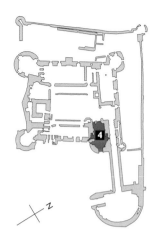

Below: Detail from the memorial window in the chapel, which contains the badges of the RAF and the various organisations involved in Radar (Radio Detection and Ranging) research. Here a Halifax bomber is shown above the circular display screen of the H2S Radar system, which aircraft V9977 was testing on its last flight

Above: Cutaway reconstruction of the gatehouse, facing east, showing the winches in the upper chamber designed to raise the two portcullises in the gate-passage below

5 GATEHOUSE UPPER ROOMS

On leaving the chapel, turn left, then go through the door immediately around the corner. This leads into a reconstructed spiral stair in the octagonal turret that projects from the south-west corner of the gatehouse. This stair gives access to the rooms over the chapel and the gate-passage, and – via a narrow corridor – to the wall-walk along the east curtain.

Carry on up the stairs as far as possible and go into the first room. This lies above the chapel, and was clearly built as a residence, as shown by the window seats and by the large fireplace, set midway along the left-hand wall. The stone smoke-hood is damaged, but the moulded corbels on which it rested still survive, though the sandstone has been badly weathered. This room might have been used by the chaplains. Alternatively, as in the gatehouses of other castles, including Caerphilly and Dover, it may have been allocated to the constable of Goodrich, the officer commanding the castle's soldiers. Square holes in the side walls suggest that there was formerly a timber partition across the end of the room, giving the occupants a degree of privacy from those passing through to the room beyond.

The smaller room beyond contains a rare survival in an English castle – evidence for the mechanism to raise and lower the portcullises in the gate-passage below. In the east wall at the far end of the room there are two rectangular recesses. These allowed turning-room for the handles of a winch, mounted on a horizontal axle which sat in the round holes in the side walls and the central column between the recesses. This mechanism was used to lift the front portcullis within the thickness of the wall with two ropes. Slightly further into the

THE SOUTH SIDE OF THE GATEHOUSE

1 Line of 13th-century pitched roof

2 Scar of a gabled roof, from the rebuilding later in the Middle Ages

3 Doors leading from the spiral stair into two galleries, inserted later in the Middle Ages

4 Fireplace to second floor, inserted later in the Middle Ages

room is the slot in the floor for the second portcullis, which originally had a winch of its own. Between the slots are two murder holes in the floor. Doors (now closed by barriers) led east into the turret room and fighting platform, now demolished, or westwards to a small latrine and originally to the north wall-walk beyond. As well as having a defensive role this room was also residential, as is shown by another large fireplace and window seats. It probably housed soldiers.

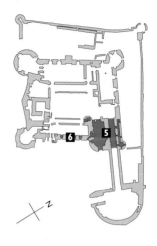

⓺ EAST WALL-WALK

Pass back through the two rooms and take the narrow passage on the left before you reach the stairs. This leads out onto the east wall-walk, from which there are good views outwards to the barbican and inwards over the castle courtyard.

The buildings at either end show traces of the lost east range of the castle which ran between them, which is archaeologically one of the most complex areas of the ruins. The marks of two phases of roof are visible in the end walls. A lower roofline, sloping down from the parapet into the interior, probably dates from the late 13th century when the east range contained only a single-storey hall. The ridged roofline above it belongs to a taller building with three storeys, which replaced the single-storey building later in the Middle Ages and provided a larger number of rooms. The floor levels of this later building are shown by the fireplace in the side of the gatehouse tower, just above the level of the wall-walk, and the inserted upper doors from the spiral stair on its left, which opened into galleries along the building's frontage, overlooking the courtyard (see illustrations).

Below: Cross-sections of the east range, facing north, showing (left) the single-storey hall of the late 13th century and (right) the three-storey range created later in the Middle Ages, with galleries overlooking the courtyard. Traces of the missing buildings are visible in the south side of the gatehouse (see photograph opposite)

Upper floor

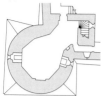

Courtyard level

Basement

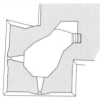

0   10 m

0   30 ft

Above: Plans of the south-east tower at upper, courtyard and basement levels
Below: A late 19th-century photograph of a graffito, now invisible, in the south-east tower at courtyard level, showing a falconer. This and other graffiti were carved by prisoners or servants, probably in the 14th century

7 SOUTH-EAST TOWER

At its south end, the wall-walk passes through the massive south-east tower, built in the late 13th century. From the modern walkway it is easy to appreciate that the round tower contained three storeys of polygonal rooms without a connecting stair: the top floor was entered either from the wall-walk (as it is now) or by a stair running up from the courtyard. The floors are missing, but can be visualised from the surviving joist-holes and stone ledges. The quality of the stonework of the walls, fireplaces, window seats and trefoil-headed washbasins at the entrances to the middle and upper floors shows that these rooms were meant for figures of some status, possibly guests. The modern nickname Prison Tower was certainly not appropriate when the tower was first built. The ground level, however, formerly contained carved graffiti, recorded in the 19th century, including figures of a falconer, various animals and the Virgin and Child; these have been provisionally dated to the late 14th century and may have been carved by prisoners or bored servants. They have mostly been lost to erosion and are now invisible.

Beyond the far doorway out of the tower there is a view over the narrow space between the keep and the remains of the south curtain wall. The square sockets and the horizontal groove cut into the south wall of the keep show that this space was once occupied by a tall building, perhaps connected with the kitchen on the far side of the keep. There are also the remains of a spiral stair added to the south-east corner of the keep, which probably led onto the south wall-walk.

8 EAST RANGE

Take the stairs down to the courtyard. At the bottom of the stairs the site of the east range can be seen on the right. An earlier building stood here, as is shown by the stonework visible from outside the castle. The large fireplace and three windows with window seats in the curtain wall date from the late 13th century, when the east range contained only a single storey. This building was certainly grand and sophisticated enough to be considered a hall, and may have been used for dining by a section of the household, perhaps servants and those of lower grade. This is suggested by the presence at the northern end of steps down into the cellar under the chapel (probably used for storage), and by the building's proximity to the garderobe tower immediately to the south. The central space with the fireplace may have been divided from the end rooms by timber partitions, now lost. At the southern end of the range are two entrances to the basement and ground floor of the south-east tower; the latter doorway was later blocked and a bread oven built immediately outside it – the lower parts of the door are still blocked with stonework.

Later in the Middle Ages, the east range was almost entirely rebuilt as a much taller building, with rooms on three levels, giving greater privacy and comfort to members of the household than the previous arrangement had allowed.

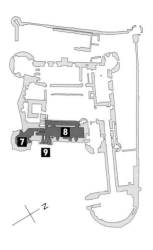

9 GARDEROBE TOWER

At the south end of the east range is the garderobe tower, added to the east curtain wall in the later Middle Ages to replace a small single latrine. This tower is one of the most remarkable features of Goodrich Castle and the survival of such a large example is extremely rare in England and Wales. It was a communal latrine for the convenience of the whole household, several of whom could use it at a time. At the level of the courtyard, three doors opened inwards into the latrine chambers, which projected beyond the line of the curtain wall in a hollow masonry buttress; each chamber may have contained more than one seat. The back wall of the tower contained two further chutes, probably ventilation shafts running upwards from the cesspit at the bottom of the buttress. Waste could be cleared out of the cess through an arched opening into the eastern ditch of the castle.

THE EAST WALL

1 Remains of three latrine chambers inside the garderobe tower

2 Outlet through which waste could be shovelled into the ditch from the garderobe tower

3 Change in the masonry, showing probable early 13th-century walling below and late 13th-century walling above

4 South-east tower

🔟 SOUTH-EAST TOWER BASEMENT AND PRISON

At the south end of the east range, the left-hand door leads down to the basement of the south-east tower, with excellent views of the tower's interior. Basement rooms of this type were often used for storage, but the socket hole in the door frame shows that this room had a drawbar to seal the original wooden door from the interior, giving a measure of privacy. This suggests that the basement may have served some other purpose, though unlike the floors above it contains no washbasin or window seats.

Returning to ground level and turning left, visitors pass the stairs down from the south-east tower and a doorway into the prison, a dark and often flooded vault, which was sealable from the outside with a drawbar, as shown by sockets in the side walls outside the stone door frame.

🔢 KEEP EXTERIOR

The keep was built in the mid-12th century, probably in the time of Richard 'Strongbow' de Clare, lord of Goodrich 1148–76, or slightly earlier. Several of its features suggest this

Above: A prisoner in leg irons, from a 15th-century manuscript
Right: The keep, seen from the east wall-walk

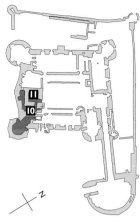

date, including the fine two-light windows facing north and west at the upper level; both are decorated with typical Romanesque chevron (zig-zag) ornament, also used on the horizontal string course around the tower, just below the windows.

The original entrance to the keep was at first-floor level, above the present entrance: it was later blocked and converted into an elegant window. The keep's lowest levels were formerly buried in an earth mound, as is clear from the rough masonry of its base, which gives way to finely dressed stone about 2m (6 ft) above the present courtyard. The four faces of the exterior are all slightly different: the two upper windows use chevron differently, the west face has no central flat pilaster buttress, and uniquely on the east face, the string course is plain rather than chevron-decorated.

The intended purpose of this and other castle keeps is a matter for debate. Its high battlements provided a perfect lookout point, and with its thick walls, relatively small windows high above the ground, and raised entrance, it would have offered some protection if the castle came under attack. Twelfth-century writers often described such towers as 'very strong', and there are numerous stories of defenders retreating inside them during sieges. The peacetime function of Goodrich's keep, however, is much less clear. Its small size compared with other keeps provided space for only one chamber on each floor: a corresponding 12th-century hall, chapel and other buildings must have stood elsewhere on the site, though later rebuilding has destroyed all trace of them. To outside observers, the tall tower made a highly visible landmark, an emblem of the lord's rank and authority.

Above: Two-light window in the west face of the keep, with chevron decoration in the jambs supporting the main arch

Below: Converted into a window in the 14th or 15th century, this opening in the north face of the keep was originally a round-headed doorway. It was the main entrance to the building in the 12th century, accessible by a wooden stair

▥ KEEP INTERIOR

The keep is now entered directly from the courtyard through a door in the north face, inserted in the 14th or 15th century. The lowest room in the keep, once lit by a narrow slit window in the east wall, was originally only entered by a stair or ladder from the room above, and was probably intended mainly for storage.

From here a modern stair leads up to a platform on the level of the entrance, though the floor has not been replaced in its entirety. From here you can see the interior of the large and elaborate entrance doorway in the north wall, later converted into a window. Though windowless and apparently without a fireplace, this room was more than 6m (20 ft) high, an impressive space in which guests could be greeted and business transacted.

Crossing to the west wall, 12th-century visitors could go through the square-headed door into the vaulted passage beyond and up a very steep, narrow spiral stair to the highest room in the tower. The floor here has also gone but visitors can look in from the staircase through the original door. With its fine windows – both with stone window seats – providing views to the west and north, this was clearly the grandest room in the keep, fit to serve as the chamber of the lord. Later in the Middle Ages another door was cut through the east wall with a bridge onto the parapet of the south-east tower.

KEEP ROOF

The stair continues to the present roof of the keep, from which there are fine views over the castle and the Wye valley.

Above: View looking north-west from the top of the keep, showing the remains of the north range and north-west tower, with the River Wye beyond

The medieval battlements are now missing, but the north wall contains some evidence for steps up to the level of the wall-walk. The inner faces of the north and south walls contain stones set at a diagonal, showing the low pitches of an early roof with a ridge running north–south. At some later stage this was replaced by a roof running at right angles to it, as is shown by the stone corbels in the east and west walls, which supported the later ridge.

12 KITCHEN

After leaving the keep, turn left round the corner of the tower. Here on the west side of the keep stood the kitchen, of which only a few traces survive at ground level. The kitchen was positioned here to serve the great hall immediately beside it. The main fireplace stood in a niche in the curtain wall, with a flagstone floor in front. Flanking it on either side and behind the keep are the remains of bread ovens, built at some time after the 13th century.

   Though only relatively small in size, the kitchen was capable of producing extremely large and complex meals. On Easter Sunday 1297, for example, the household at Goodrich ended its Lenten fast with '3 quarters of beef and 1½ bacons, 1½ unsalted pigs, half a boar, half a salmon, all from the castle's store, half a carcass of beef costing 10 shillings, mutton at 15 pence, 9 kid at 3s 8d, 17 capons and hens at 2s 7d, 2 veal calves at 2s 6d, 600 eggs at 2 shillings, pigeons at 2 pence with 24 other pigeons from stores in Shrivenham, cheese at 4 pence and a halfpenny for transport by boat, all told, 22s 6d halfpenny'.

Above: An artist's impression of the kitchen at Goodrich. The positions of its hearth, ovens and water trough can be identified in the remains, but the building only survives to a few courses above ground level

Below: A baker placing loaves in an oven, from an illuminated manuscript of about 1340

Above: The high table of a hall in the mid-14th century, from the Luttrell Psalter. The lord sits in the centre, with members of his family and two Dominican friars, against a backdrop with the lord's heraldic insignia. Countess Joan de Valence's household accounts describe similar scenes of the Countess dining with her family, important visitors and even a party of friars in 1296 and 1297

Facing page, top: The paired doors leading from the ground floor of the south-west tower into the great hall beyond, seen from the tower basement. The ground floor was formerly partitioned, serving as the buttery (for dispensing drink) and pantry (for bread). The upper doorway has a distinctive 'shouldered' head

Facing page, below: Plans of the south-west tower at upper, courtyard and basement levels. The shaded area in the basement plan marks the buried foundations of an earlier tower

🅱 GREAT HALL

Turn left on leaving the kitchen to enter the great hall, the focal building of Goodrich Castle, running along the western side of the courtyard. This was the centre of household activity and the setting for feasts and other large gatherings of the household and guests. The four doors in the south end led into the south-west tower beyond. The two on the right communicated with the buttery and pantry on the tower's ground floor, where wine and bread were stored and served. The door to their left led down to the cellar below them, while the stairs on the far left led to the upper floor of the tower. The slightly sloping scar on the wall above the doors indicates that the hall roof was almost flat. Its main ceiling beams and arch braces formerly rested on the two tiers of moulded stone supports or corbels visible in the side walls.

Unlike many halls, which had a traditional open hearth in the centre of the floor, that at Goodrich had an enormous fireplace in the western wall. This is flanked by three tall windows running the whole height of the room. The windows on the other side were smaller and set high up to clear the covered passage around the courtyard beyond. Below these windows is a stone bench running along the wall, which doubtless originally had a long table in front. The table of the lord and most important members of the household would have been at the north end of the hall, probably on a raised dais. At a later stage, a gallery was built over this end, entered through a high door in the centre of the north wall.

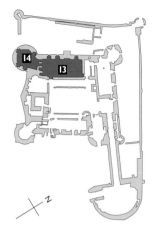

4 SOUTH-WEST TOWER

At the south end of the hall, take the flight of stairs down
into the basement of the three-storey south-west tower. The
floor above was formerly divided by a timber partition into a
buttery and pantry, each containing one window with stone
window seats and one arrowloop. Only the upper floor was
solely residential, with a washbasin and a large hooded
fireplace. This room was entered by a covered stairway rising
from the south end of the hall, a sign that it was intended for
an important figure – perhaps a guest or one of the owner's
family, such as Aymer de Valence (d. 1324), later lord of
Goodrich, who stayed here with his mother, the Countess
Joan, for long periods in 1296–7.

This tower has different architectural details from the other
towers at Goodrich and was probably built slightly later. This is
most evident internally from the 'shouldered' heads over an
upper door and the arrowloops on the middle floor, and in
the flatter arches of the wide embrasures on all floors. These
features are particularly associated with the royal castles built
by King Edward I in north Wales in the 1280s, though they
also occur elsewhere. They appear at ground and upper levels
in this tower but only at the highest levels in the castle's other
buildings, suggesting that this tower was only begun as other
parts of the castle were nearing completion.

In the tower's basement are the foundations (now reburied)
of an earlier, thinner tower. This may have been built in the
early 13th century by William Marshal, as he had earlier built
similar round towers at nearby Chepstow Castle. The lower
parts of the east curtain wall may also date from this time.

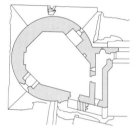

Upper floor

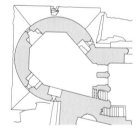

Courtyard level

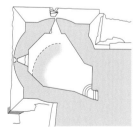

Basement

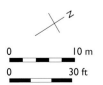

0		10 m
0		30 ft

Above: Cutaway reconstructions of the north range at Goodrich (right) and the Great Tower of nearby Chepstow Castle (left). The twin arches at Goodrich may have been modelled on those built in the 1230s at Chepstow

Bottom: A trefoil-headed basin in the basement of the north range, beside the entrance from the outer ward. A surviving pipe brought water from the castle's well in the courtyard. Other washbasins can be seen around the castle, often beside entrance doorways

🔢 LOBBY AND NORTH RANGE VESTIBULE

Return to the great hall, where you will find a small door at its far end. This door is not an original feature but was broken through the wall, probably in the 14th century; originally, access between the great hall and the tower was via the covered passageway around the courtyard. The doorway leads into the remains of a small lobby connecting the hall to the north range and the north-west tower, which may originally have housed the private quarters of the lord and his family. With its stone bench along the south wall, the lobby served as a waiting room for visitors to the inner rooms of the noble household. It now preserves evidence of a less grand use: graffiti, scratched in the plaster by visitors to the ruined and overgrown castle in the 19th century (see page 45).

After ruination in the Civil War of the 1640s and two serious falls of stonework in 1919, the remains here are too fragmentary to be reconstructed with certainty, and they are further confused by evidence of alterations in the later Middle Ages. But in the late 13th century there was clearly an upper floor over the lobby, which has been interpreted as a private chapel on the basis of a surviving piscina and possible sedile high in its south wall, above the door to the hall. This chapel would have lain close to the principal apartments in the north range, but the details of the layout remain hard to visualise, especially the location of staircases which must have led to the upper floors in this corner of the castle. The adjoining vestibule and north-west tower have largely disappeared, but some idea of their former grandeur can be appreciated by looking through the doorway to the left of the stairs which lead down into the basement. In particular, the square sockets for the floor joists show that the rooms on this level were extremely tall, forming a most imposing entrance to the private apartments of the owner of Goodrich.

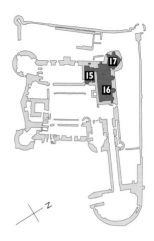

16 NORTH RANGE

From the lobby take the narrow stair down into the basement of the north range, sometimes called the north hall or solar block. This building is as remarkable as it is hard to interpret. It was clearly of high architectural quality, but some of its layout and its original function are unclear – only two walls survive above basement level. The range, with two elegant window seats at courtyard level and one in the basement below, was built in the late 13th century. It is connected by two enormous arches at its west end to the high vestibule that led into the north-west tower: these arches may have been modelled on a screen of paired arches at nearby Chepstow Castle, owned by the earls of Norfolk at the time Goodrich was being rebuilt. The south and east walls of the range are completely missing above the basement, and no fireplace survives on either level. In the south-east corner of the basement is a well-preserved 13th-century basin with a spout above and a drain in the sink below.

The location of this range within the castle suggests that, in its early phases, the upper floor served as a private 'solar' or great chamber for the higher levels of the household. The stonework above the arches, however, also contains evidence that in the late Middle Ages the roof of the range was heightened and a third floor inserted – perhaps to add extra bedrooms – level with the heads of the two arches, and completely altering its original function.

17 NORTH-WEST TOWER

From the basement of the north range, you can reach the lowest floor of the north-west tower, or Lady Tower, via the vestibule basement. This tower, once similar externally to the massive south-east tower with its high pyramid-shaped spur buttresses, was brought down by concentrated mortar fire during the Civil War siege of 1646. Today, apart from two thin stacks of masonry, it only survives at basement level. Even so, enough remains to suggest the great height of the rooms and the unusually good facilities in this tower, which together with the north range once contained the castle's most important accommodation. Uniquely for Goodrich even its basement contained window seats and a fireplace, so that with its surviving latrine in the vestibule (corresponding to another at higher level), this room could serve as living space rather than storage. There must have been similar and better fittings on the two floors above, though all trace of these has been lost.

Below: The remains of the paired arches between the north range (foreground) and the vestibule and north-west tower beyond

Above: The remains of the outer curtain wall, which formerly protected the north and west flanks of the castle, and was largely destroyed in the 17th century
Below: The site of the stables, burned down by Parliamentarian soldiers during a night raid in March 1646. Beyond the stables are the remains of the great hall and south-west tower

🔳 OUTER WARD

Pass back through the north range basement and turn left through the small doorway in the north-east corner. This postern door, once sealed by a small portcullis operated from the floor above, leads to the outer ward. Once outside the wall, turn left: from here it is possible to walk around the complete circuit of the outer ward and ditch. (This involves a steep climb at the end over the bedrock in the eastern ditch, and may become hazardous in wet weather; if it is wet, you are advised to retrace your steps to this doorway.)

Surrounded by a ditch cut from the rock on the south and east sides, Goodrich Castle had neither the need nor the space for a second curtain wall around the whole circuit, like Caerphilly or the better-known concentric castles of Edward I at the Tower of London and at Rhuddlan, Harlech and Beaumaris in Wales. To the north and west, however, the sloping ground was cut away and a second wall with turrets was built on a level terrace. This operation was almost certainly carried out in the late 13th century for William de Valence or his widow, the Countess Joan. Surviving traces of a cross-shaped arrowloop in the turret at its north-west angle

are similar to those of the castle's south-west tower. The outer wall and its towers only survive as low footings. Before the Civil War, they were described as 'very high'; they were damaged in 1646 during an attack on the castle's stables and reduced in height afterwards to make the castle less defensible in future.

From the outer ward the damage which the castle suffered in 1646 during the Civil War is particularly clear, especially the almost complete destruction of the north-west tower, on which the besiegers had concentrated their attack. The walls to the right of the tower have also suffered badly from the loss of facing stone, collapsing masonry and heavy-handed repairs in the 20th century, which have obscured much of the evidence for the castle's shape and development.

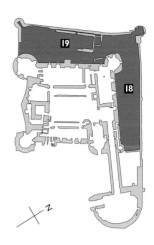

🔟 STABLES

Midway along the west side of the outer ward, cobbled floors and low stone footings are survivals of the castle's stables, probably dating to the 17th century. Given the difficulty of descending to this level from the barbican, the medieval stables probably lay on higher ground outside the castle. These later stables were large enough for about 60 horses, though 17th-century descriptions mention higher numbers.

The stables were destroyed in the early hours of 10 March 1646, during a raid by Parliamentarian soldiers. In darkness and under cover of a diversionary attack on the gates, the raiders climbed over the outer curtain wall and dug a hole in it. They captured the horses and led them away, then set the stables on fire. This action, three months before the final siege of the castle, was a complete success and was widely reported in Parliamentarian accounts (see page 43).

The tall windows with horizontal bars (transoms) in the west curtain wall above the stables gave light into the great hall, integrally built with this part of the castle's defences. At the south-west tower, the height of the moulded horizontal string course is noticeably different from that of the west wall. This, and the fact that its supporting buttresses terminate much lower than the high pyramidal spurs of the other towers, suggests that the south-west tower was probably rebuilt a little later than the rest of the castle. Nevertheless, it was built soon enough to retain similarity both to other late 13th-century buildings, like Castell Coch (finished in about 1277) and Marten's Tower at Chepstow (finished in 1293), and, in features like the rectangular frames around windows, to other parts of Goodrich as well.

At the foot of the south-west tower, much confused by repairs made in 1925, are the treads of a spiral stair, now disappearing into the base. These probably led into the tower's basement, where a large area of inserted masonry covers a likely postern doorway.

Above: The south-west tower at Goodrich (top) has spur buttresses similar to those of Marten's Tower at Chepstow Castle (above), completed in 1293

Above: The south side of Goodrich Castle seen from across the rock-cut ditch, showing the south-west tower (left), south-east tower (right) and keep (centre)

20 DITCH

The remains of a small gate at the south-west corner mark the end of the outer ward and the beginning of the rock-cut ditch which surrounds the castle's south and east sides.

Continue round the circuit below the south curtain with its angled faces and the south-east tower. The ditch then turns left (north) to run along the east front of the castle. From here there is a good view of the garderobe tower and particularly the opening at its base, through which waste could be shovelled into the ditch. The stretch of curtain wall to the right of the garderobe tower shows a rare trace of the castle which may have been built by William Marshal in the early 13th century. The stonework below the rectangular windows is clearly different in character from that above, and contains the bottoms of two narrow slit openings, cut off and blocked when the upper parts of the wall were rebuilt for the de Valences (see photograph on page 15).

If conditions permit, you can climb up to the arches under the entrance causeway. (Alternatively, if the rocky slope is slippery, you can retrace your steps back around the outside of the castle to the postern door.) Both these arches were later blocked with masonry, though the right-hand arch has since been reopened. This blocking, and the gate at the south-west corner of the castle, theoretically sealed off the outer ward from the unenclosed areas of the ditch. From under the causeway you can see in the wall underneath the gatehouse three slots, now blocked, which allowed the counterweights for the original pivoting drawbridge to swing down when the drawbridge was to be raised.

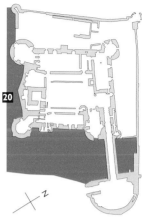

Beyond the causeway the route leads past the base of the small north turret of the gatehouse. The building here shows the influence of many developments in 'military' castle architecture during the century before its construction. At the same time, the outstanding quality of the turret's stonework, notably the way in which the flat surfaces of the spur buttresses turn into the curvature of the drum tower, shows an attention to detail more usually associated with great churches and palaces than with castles. This combination of military strength and fine architecture is characteristic of Goodrich Castle.

Above: The arches of the causeway linking the barbican to the main gatehouse. Both arches were blocked soon after construction: stone walling survives in the left-hand arch

THE UNDERSIDE OF THE CAUSEWAY

1 Pit in the roadway above, formerly covered by the 13th-century drawbridge and now by a fixed bridge

2 Site of the axle on which the bridge formerly pivoted

3 Three slots for the counterweights of the drawbridge, later filled with stonework

History

Goodrich Castle was owned successively by the Marshal, Valence and Talbot families, many of whom were significant figures in war and national politics. Despite its border setting, the castle led a largely peaceful existence until it was besieged and captured by Parliamentarians during the Civil War.

READING THE HISTORY

This section describes the history of Goodrich Castle up to the present. It contains features on one of the castle's owners, William de Valence (page 34) and his Countess, Joan (page 36).

'GODRIC'S CASTLE'

For many centuries there has been an important crossing point on the River Wye close to Goodrich Castle, creating one of the major routes between England and Wales. The area has been occupied for at least 1,000 and perhaps as many as 2,000 years – it is possible that earthworks around the castle were part of a hillfort dating from the Iron Age (about 800 BC – AD 43). Human burials, perhaps from an early Christian cemetery, have also been found south-east of the castle close to the present path, and crop-marks in the fields show that other buildings stood in the same area.

The history of the castle itself begins soon after the Norman Conquest. In Domesday Book of 1086 an entry records that land in *Hulla* – which may be Howle, 5km (3 miles) from the castle, or may simply mean 'hill' – belonged to Godric Mappeson. The name Godric suggests that he was an Englishman rather than a Norman, though nothing more is known about him. Domesday does not mention that his estate included a castle, but by 1101–2 other documents show that 'Godric's Castle' was already in existence. With changes to the spelling, this has been its name ever since.

Whether or not it stood on this site, nothing of the first castle survives, and neither it nor its builder played an important part in local politics. Godric had probably died before 1100, and the castle passed to William fitz Baderon, thought to be his son-in-law, and thence to William's son Baderon in the 1120s.

In the shifting power politics of Herefordshire in the 1130s, King Stephen (reigned 1135–54) was hard pressed to maintain the loyalty of local barons against his rival claimant to the throne, the Empress Matilda (d. 1167), daughter of Henry I. Goodrich, with the Wye crossing under its control, had particular strategic value. In about 1138, Stephen engineered the transfer of Goodrich to Gilbert fitz Gilbert de Clare (d. 1148), and promoted him earl of Pembroke. It is likely that Gilbert maintained Goodrich in the cause of Stephen, while almost all other noblemen in Herefordshire transferred their allegiance to the empress during the civil war that followed.

Having supported Stephen with his father, Gilbert's son, Richard 'Strongbow' de Clare (d. 1176), who succeeded in 1148, found himself out of favour when the empress's son took the throne as Henry II (reigned 1154–89). Richard later achieved fame as conqueror of Ireland, to which he sailed, in defiance of royal instructions, in 1170, at the invitation of an exiled Irish king. From the style of its architecture it seems likely that the keep at Goodrich was built during a refortification of the castle by either Gilbert or Richard de Clare, or even in the early years of Henry II's reign, when Richard had forfeited the earldom of Pembroke and was politically in the wilderness. Unfortunately nothing else

Above: King Stephen (reigned 1135–54), from a late 13th-century manuscript. The de Clares at Goodrich were the most important local supporters of the king over his rival claimant to the throne, the Empress Matilda

Facing page: Detail from an engraving of Goodrich Castle by Samuel and Nathaniel Buck, made in 1731, showing the gatehouse and causeway

Below: Effigy of William Marshal I (d. 1219) in the Temple Church, London. 'The best knight in all the world', even according to an enemy, William acquired Goodrich in 1204 and probably rebuilt parts of the curtain wall in stone

survives of the castle in which the keep was built: it was probably a fairly small enclosure, perhaps with only earth and timber defences, and certainly with other domestic buildings such as a hall, kitchen and chapel. Though it contains several fine architectural details such as the windows, moulded string courses and a fine doorway, the keep at Goodrich was only small in size: it looked imposing from a distance, but would not have cost its builder too much money.

Richard de Clare had great military successes in Ireland in the 1170s with the capture of Dublin, further arousing Henry II's suspicion, though he later fought for Henry in Normandy; he died in Dublin in 1176. His adventures were commemorated in the Norman French poem, *The Song of Dermot and the Earl*. Since both his son and daughter were children when he died, Richard's estate reverted to the Crown. Goodrich would remain in royal hands until 1204.

WILLIAM MARSHAL AND HIS SONS

Though the Crown withheld the titles and manors of Richard Strongbow and only released them in stages, the right of inheritance passed to Richard's daughter, Isabella (d. 1220). On his accession in 1189, Richard I confirmed the promise made by his father Henry II that Isabella should marry a knight of the royal household, William Marshal (d. 1219). William came from relatively humble origins but rose in the service of princes and kings to become one of the greatest and most respected soldiers and statesmen of his day. At his marriage he received the border castles at Chepstow and Usk, undertaking massive and innovative extensions to the defences at both sites. Ten years later, King John (reigned 1199–1216) granted him the prestigious earldom of Pembroke. Finally, in 1204, he was awarded Goodrich Castle, possibly in compensation for losing his estates in Normandy to the French who annexed the duchy of Normandy in that year, separating it from England for the first time since 1066.

William Marshal probably took measures to modernise the buildings at Goodrich around this time, although no documentary evidence exists for this. Surviving work at his castles at Pembroke, Usk and Chepstow shows that he was among the greatest castle builders of his age, and if much of Goodrich Castle was in earth and timber in 1204, it is entirely likely that he would have upgraded its defences. The lower courses of the east curtain wall and the foundations of an earlier round tower discovered in 1925 underneath the present south-west tower may date to this period.

The last years of King John's reign were marked by violence and disorder, as the king tried to repudiate the terms of Magna Carta, which a number of English barons had forced him to accept in 1215. When Prince Louis of France invaded southern England at the invitation of the rebel barons, William

Marshal was pre-eminent among the loyalists who resisted the French. After King John's death in October 1216, William supervised a hasty coronation at Gloucester for the nine-year-old Henry III (reigned 1216–72), knighting the young king himself. In the event, the banquet after the ceremony was interrupted by news that Goodrich Castle needed reinforcement against a Welsh attack, which William was forced to repel. William later played a central role in the expulsion of the French, fighting with distinction in the crucial battle in the streets of Lincoln on 20 May 1217 (at the age of 72), and served as regent of England in the earliest years of Henry III's minority. He died in 1219, joining the crusading order of the Knights Templar on his deathbed.

William and Isabella had five sons, all of whom succeeded as earl of Pembroke; all died childless in their turn, leaving titles and estates to the next brother. On William's death, his eldest son, also named William (d. 1231), inherited the earldom of Pembroke and title to much of the estate; Goodrich itself was ceded to the fourth son, Walter (d. 1245), who lived in the castle for much of his life. In 1231 the second son, Richard (d. 1234), succeeded his brother. He led the opposition in 1233 to powerful foreigners in Henry III's court and made an alliance with the Welsh, for which the king ordered Goodrich Castle to be besieged. Whether or not actual fighting ensued, the castle was made to submit to the royal lieutenant. Richard withdrew to Ireland where he was killed in battle the following year. The third son, Gilbert, was quickly reconciled with the king and inherited the earldom, but he died in a tournament accident in 1241, after

Above: Chepstow Castle, overlooking the Wye close to its estuary. Much of the curtain wall and several towers were built by William Marshal in the late 12th and early 13th centuries

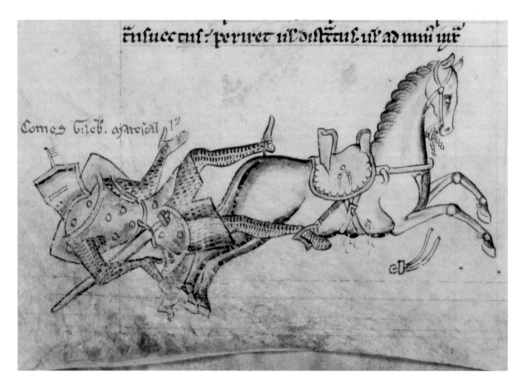

Above: Illustration from the Greater Chronicle of Matthew Paris, a monk of St Albans, showing the fatal fall of Gilbert Marshal in a tournament at Hertford on 27 June 1241. Matthew reports a suspicion that his harness had been tampered with

which Walter finally inherited the title to his home at Goodrich. Walter is known to have lived at Goodrich for some time, although he also undertook military campaigns elsewhere, for example in Gascony in 1244. He had fallen ill by July 1245 and died at Goodrich on 24 November that year, according to 19th-century tradition, in the keep itself. The final brother, Anselm, died about a month later, and so did not live long enough to be officially confirmed in the earldom.

THE DE VALENCES AND THE REBUILDING OF GOODRICH CASTLE

As there were no surviving male heirs, the estate was divided between the five daughters of William Marshal and their descendants. Goodrich passed briefly to John de Munchensi, son of the late Joan (d. 1234), William Marshal's youngest daughter. John died childless in 1247, and the castle passed to his sister, Joan de Munchensi (d. 1307). In this year, Henry III arranged Joan's marriage to a young knight from the area of Poitiers, William de Valence (d. 1296), Henry III's half-brother from his mother's second marriage (see page 34). Under William and Joan de Valence, Goodrich Castle would enjoy a new period of favour and renovation.

The buildings of Goodrich Castle as we see them today have been variously dated to the late 13th and early 14th centuries and attributed to William de Valence, his widow, Joan or his son Aymer (d. 1324). An early date for the rebuilding is likely for several reasons. First, royal records mention gifts of timber from the Forest of Dean explicitly 'for works at Godric's Castle' as early as 1261, when William was generally consolidating his estates after an enforced exile, and again in the early 1280s and in 1293. In 1296 royal workmen were documented as staying nearby, presumably assisting with building works at Goodrich as a gift from Edward I to his uncle William, though in fact William died shortly afterwards. There could have been several pauses in construction within this long period: William's resources must have been committed elsewhere during civil wars in the mid-1260s, in Edward I's Welsh wars of 1277–7 and 1282–3, and from 1286 until 1289 when he was with the king and queen in Gascony. Second, when William's widow Countess Joan stayed at Goodrich in 1296 and 1297 for several months, the castle was evidently not a building site and was already able to accommodate the whole household of about 200 people. Almost certainly the castle's apartments were already finished by then.

Finally, architecturally the new buildings at Goodrich are similar to castles modernised by both relations and rivals of the de Valences which are known to date from the last quarter of the 13th century. For example, the high spur buttresses on the south-east and north-west towers and the gatehouse are very like examples at Caerphilly (1270s) or the chapel at Kidwelly (1280s or 1290s), which Edward I granted to William in 1283. The slightly different base of the south-west tower resembles those at Castell Coch (about 1277) or Marten's Tower at Chepstow (finished in 1293). The barbican is almost identical in plan to that built for Edward I at the Tower of London between 1275 and 1281. Most of the surviving buildings are therefore likely to date from between the 1270s and the 1290s.

Above: Polygonal towers on the eastern dam of Caerphilly Castle, built in the 1270s for Gilbert de Clare, earl of Gloucester (1243–95). Similar high spur buttresses can be seen at Goodrich and at Kidwelly, both belonging to William de Valence

Below: Masons and labourers building the Tower of Babel, from a manuscript of the mid-13th century. Goodrich Castle was rebuilt about this time, no doubt using similar methods

William de Valence, 'Earl' of Pembroke

The half-brother of Henry III, William was one of the leading figures of his time

Above: The Wye valley region, showing the locations of castles
Below: The tomb of William de Valence in Westminster Abbey, with a copper gilt effigy decorated in Limoges enamel

William de Valence, for whom Goodrich Castle was rebuilt in the second half of the 13th century, was half-brother to Henry III and uncle to Edward I, and in his own right, one of the leading political figures of his time. He was the son of Isabella of Angoulême, widow of King John, and her second husband, Hugues de Lusignan, count of La Marche.

Little is known of William's early life in Gascony, but in 1247 Henry III invited him to England, arranging his marriage to Joan, heiress of William Marshal, through whom he inherited the lordship of Pembroke and several manors including Goodrich. He was never formally created earl by Henry III or Edward I, but the title was used informally both by William himself and others. Other great magnates owned castles in the area including the earls of Lancaster (Grosmont and Skenfrith), Norfolk (Chepstow) and Gloucester (Caerphilly, Usk and Castell Coch, all to the west) as well as the king himself (Hereford and St Briavels).

Considered a foreign upstart by many English nobles, William supported Henry III against Simon de Montfort and his adherents; he endured exile and forfeiture of his estates, and fought for the king at the battles of Lewes and Evesham and at the siege of Kenilworth. In 1270 he accompanied the future Edward I on crusade to Acre, but returned early to safeguard his lands from his rival, the earl of Gloucester. He fought again for Edward I as commander in the southern army against the Welsh in 1277–8, supervising the construction of a royal castle at Aberystwyth, and captured the Welsh stronghold of Castell y Bere in 1282–3. He later undertook further military and diplomatic missions in Gascony and Flanders.

In 1296, wounded in a skirmish, William was carried from Dover to his manor at Brabourne in Kent, where he died. Goodrich Castle passed in dower to his widow and in 1307 to his son Aymer.

COUNTESS JOAN AND HER HOUSEHOLD

Countess Joan lived at Goodrich for long periods after the death of her husband William de Valence in 1296. Three remarkable manuscripts have survived in the National Archives recording her household expenses for the year beginning 29 September 1296, which includes two long stays at Goodrich Castle between 18 November 1296 and 7 May 1297, and again in September of the same year. The accounts provide a rare insight into the personnel and activities of a great castle household at the end of the 13th century.

The Countess's household fluctuated between 122 and 196 people. She was often joined by her daughter Isabel, her son Aymer and his first wife Beatrice, and by eminent guests including the young Gilbert de Clare and his household, the lady of Raglan Castle and the prioress of Aconbury. They were attended by the important officers of the household: the steward (the senior officer, responsible for the running of the household) and the treasurer (who oversaw the household's finances), and in the chapel a staff of several clerks, who sang the religious services and also undertook more worldly duties. The regular travelling of the Countess's entourage required a number of grooms and coachmen, while cooks and porters might also have travelled with the main party. There was also a staff permanently based at Goodrich under the command of the castle's constable, who maintained the security of the fortress. At the bottom of the hierarchy were 20 poor people, dependent on the Countess's charity. It is hard to see how all of these people could be housed at once in the relatively small castle at Goodrich. This household was small, however, in comparison to that which travelled with the king of the day, Edward I, which was sometimes twice this size.

Above: A scene in a lady's chamber, from the mid-14th-century Luttrell Psalter. The casket beside the kneeling maid is a simpler version of the Valence Casket (left)

Left: A casket for jewels or other valuables, probably made in the time of William de Valence or Countess Joan. The presence of the Valence arms together with those of England, Brittany, Brabant and Lucy has led to its being named the Valence Casket. It is now in the Victoria and Albert Museum

Countess Joan's Accounts

As these extracts show, the surviving accounts of Countess Joan's household for 1296–7 provide detailed insights into many aspects of life at Goodrich: the names of relatives, guests and servants, where and how they travelled, what they ate and where it was bought, and what furnishings and clothes they needed

Below: The covered carriage of a queen or great lady, drawn by five horses and accompanied by outriders, from the 14th-century Luttrell Psalter. The Countess Joan's carriage and several of her horses were kept at nearby Moreton Valence while she resided at Goodrich

18 November 1296, the day of the Countess's arrival at Goodrich:
Item 10 shillings 6 pence in procuring 3 carts to transport the mistress's property by road. Item 6 pence for a horse to carry the mistress's money by road. Item 2 shillings, 5 pence for 8 horses and 4 carters, loaned by the abbot of Gloucester and the abbot of Nutley for transporting the mistress's property by road, staying a night across the river Wye, unable to get across. Item 3 shillings and 6 pence for the 4-horse cart of the abbot of Nutley, taking 3 days to return from Goodrich Castle to Nutley, and a gift of 6 pence from the mistress to the carters. Item a gift of 6 pence from the mistress for the abbot of Gloucester's 4-horse cart on its return journey, and 1 penny for the wages of a boy conveying the mistress to Richard de Moreton. Item 16 pence to John the baker for 8 days travelling from Exning to Goodrich Castle to bake bread there before the mistress's arrival, and 16 pence to Isaac [of the kitchen] travelling to Goodrich Castle to prepare the larder there.

2 pence to buy 5 frames for the pavilion over the mistress's bed
4 pence for 2 lights for the chamber of the mistress and Beatrice, her daughter-in-law, for the week
7½ pence for the expenses of the clerk Phillip for travelling to Chepstow to buy salt fish and herring
1 penny for a lock for the door of the building where the horses' feed is kept
6 pence for buying a storm lantern for the kitchen window
4 pounds, 5 shillings and 6 pence for 114 pounds of wax bought at Monmouth by master Thomas the Chaplain at 9 pence per pound
8 pence in expenses for Hamo the coachman, travelling to Gloucester to bring a man to mend the mistress's carriage
8 pence for making 2 surplices for the mistress's chapel
18 pence to the chaplain for making wax tapers for the chapel

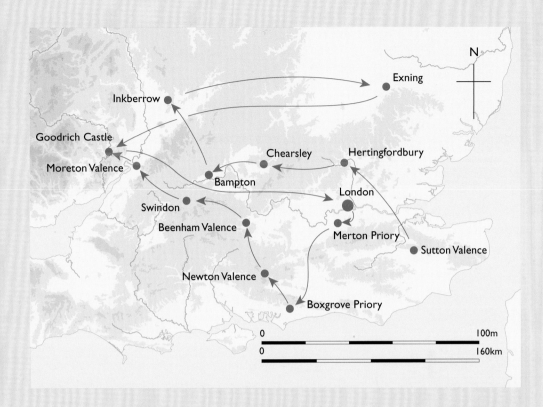

A halfpenny for mending the door to the chapel where oats are kept [*This was written soon after the Countess's return in September 1297; perhaps there had been no time to tidy the whole of the castle before her arrival.*]

Receiving a footwear allowance for the Easter Term [*1297*]: The chapel clerk, Humphrey [of the mistress's chamber], John of the Wardrobe, Richard the usher, the mistress's laundress, Walter the farrier, John Bendogeda, John Cely, Richard the Sauserer, John the Baker, the mistress's herald, Isaac [of the kitchen], Richard of Stanes, John the mistress's palfreyman [*who looked after her palfrey or riding-horse*], Hec the coachman, Burgeys, Adam the carter, the groom of Edward Burnel, Davy the coachman and John the carter, one rate between them, a half-rate to Henry Pendyn.

Above: Map showing the movements of Countess Joan and her household between May 1296 and September 1297. She stayed at several properties for long periods, including five and a half months at Goodrich Castle, two months at her manor in Swindon, and two months with her daughter Agnes at Hertingfordbury. She also briefly stayed as a guest at monasteries along the way

Above: Detail from the tomb of Aymer de Valence in Westminster Abbey, showing the earl armed and on horseback
Below: Detail from a late 18th-century engraving showing the remains of Flanesford Priory, close to the Wye below Goodrich Castle. The priory was endowed by Richard Talbot in 1343, and was the last foundation of Augustinian canons in England

AYMER DE VALENCE

Aymer de Valence, who inherited Goodrich Castle in 1307 from his mother, Countess Joan, was one of the last generation of nobles to hold significant estates in France as well as England. Like his father, Aymer played an important role in English politics, mostly as a supporter of the monarch, although Edward II (reigned 1307–27) did little to merit his loyalty. Though he had stayed at Goodrich during his mother's lifetime, he was frequently called away on royal business. The once-accepted idea that much of Goodrich Castle was built during his period of ownership now seems less likely: the castle he inherited was almost certainly complete.

Aymer had served on missions abroad with his father and not long after receiving the earldom of Pembroke in 1307, he was involved in negotiations for the marriage of Edward II and Princess Isabella of France. He soon quarrelled with Piers Gaveston, the king's unpopular favourite, and found himself in a faction agitating for reform. However, he did not assent to the capture and execution of Gaveston by the earls of Warwick and Lancaster, and later transferred his support to the king's party. In 1314, as the king's lieutenant in Scotland, he helped Edward II to safety after the calamitous defeat at Bannockburn.

Personal disaster overtook Aymer in 1317 when he was returning from a mission to the Pope in Avignon. He was captured and imprisoned by a French nobleman, who believed Aymer owed him money, and ransomed for the enormous sum of £10,400. The repayments ruined him financially for the remainder of his life. Though he married twice, Aymer had no heir, and at his death the lordship of Goodrich passed to his young niece, Elizabeth Comyn. During her minority the castle was again taken into Crown custody.

THE TALBOTS

At the time of Aymer's death, real power at the court of Edward II lay with his then favourites, the father and son both named Hugh le Despenser. The Despensers pressured Elizabeth Comyn to surrender her various possessions to them, kidnapping her and holding her prisoner, until in March 1325 she finally released Goodrich to the younger Despenser. Shortly afterwards Elizabeth married Richard Talbot, second Lord Talbot (d. 1356), who in 1326 seized the castle in her name, probably before the Despensers were themselves forced from power.

Richard Talbot was a courtier and a distinguished soldier, fighting in Scotland and in the Hundred Years' War in France. At Goodrich, having briefly established a community of priests to sing mass in the castle chapel in 1338, in 1343 he endowed a small priory of Augustinian canons at Flanesford, immediately beside the river crossing below the castle. One of the buildings, thought to be the prior's lodging and

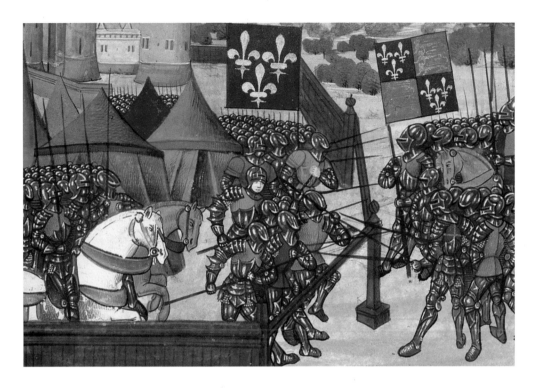

guesthouse, has survived in private ownership, though no trace can be seen of a priory church.

In 1402 the security of the marches was threatened by the Welsh rebellion led by Owain Glyn Dŵr. Orders were issued for the safeguard of Goodrich Castle, and Welsh forces invaded the area in June 1404. In March 1405 the young Gilbert, fifth Lord Talbot, who had served in the army of the prince of Wales (later Henry V), was instrumental in repelling another incursion. In 1408–9 Gilbert was fighting in north Wales, recovering Harlech Castle from Glyn Dŵr's rebels. Most famously, he accompanied Henry V to Normandy in 1415, and died in Rouen in 1418. Gilbert's brother John, 'the terror of the French', who had served in Ireland, inherited Goodrich in 1421. He spent much of his life fighting in France, being rewarded in 1442 with the earldom of Shrewsbury, and certainly saw little of Goodrich. He died in battle in 1453 trying to save the town of Castillon from a French siege.

Architectural evidence suggests that some of the visible alterations to Goodrich Castle were carried out under the Talbots in the 15th century. These include the new internal gallery at the west end of the chapel, the extension of the accommodation for retainers and servants in the east range, and the creation of a further storey above the more prestigious accommodation in the north range, communicating with the chapel. We do not know which of the castle's owners had these works carried out. For most of the 15th century the Talbots were either heavily involved in warfare and politics elsewhere, or the castle was being held by outsiders while the heir was still a minor.

Above: A late 15th-century manuscript illustration of the siege of Castillon-sur-Dordogne in 1453, at which John Talbot was killed

Below: Detail of a corbel in the chapel, carved as an angel bearing a shield. This was added by the Talbots, probably in the first half of the 15th century, to support a beam (see page 11)

Above: Graffito, now lost, from the south-east or 'prison tower', showing a hart and a swan. These are often dated to the 14th century, though the tower was still used as a prison in the 1530s

Below: A chalk drawing of George Talbot, sixth earl of Shrewsbury, by a 16th-century French artist. George Talbot was entrusted with guarding Mary Queen of Scots and spent most of his time away from Goodrich

THE EARLS OF SHREWSBURY

It was not only the demands of military campaigns – whether overseas or, during the 15th century, the Wars of the Roses between the rival royal houses of York and Lancaster – that kept successive lords of Goodrich away from the castle. They were also called elsewhere by the greater size and attraction of their other residences, especially the castle and manor of Sheffield in Yorkshire. When John Talbot, second earl of Shrewsbury, died in 1460 fighting for Henry VI at the battle of Northampton, his son, another John (d. 1473), inherited at the age of 11. Goodrich was granted by the new Yorkist king Edward IV (1461–83) to William Herbert of Raglan, who was made earl of Pembroke in 1468, so briefly reinstating the connection between Goodrich and Pembroke; Goodrich finally came into the third earl of Shrewsbury's hands in 1469. When he died four years later, once again the heir, George, was a minor, and Goodrich Castle was placed in the care of receivers. George, fourth earl of Shrewsbury (1468–1538), finally took possession of his lands in November 1485. His main interests were at court and in Sheffield, but he held several judicial posts in the Goodrich area and this may lie behind John Leland's observation in the 1530s that 'they carry their prisoners to Castel Goderyce … belonging to the Earl of Shrewsbury'. Some of the castle buildings must have served as a prison for the local courts at this time.

During the tenure of Francis Talbot, the fifth earl (1538–60) and George, the sixth earl (1560–90), the pattern of absenteeism continued. George in particular was occupied with the safe custody of Mary Queen of Scots between 1569 and 1584, and spent much of his time in Sheffield. Goodrich continued to provide an income from timber, the Wye fisheries and ironworking; the weirs of the fisheries sometimes flooded, causing problems for the forges. The estate courts exacted fines for misdemeanours: the castle ditch was occasionally used as a pound for confiscated cattle.

Earl George's second wife, whom he married in 1568, was the wealthy and three-times married Elizabeth St Loe, better known as Bess of Hardwick. A convenient double marriage linked the earl's son Gilbert and daughter Grace to Bess's daughter Mary and son Henry. Initially it was intended that Henry should occupy Goodrich, but in the event, it was Gilbert and Mary who moved there in 1575, with Gilbert serving as his father's steward. Gilbert almost certainly modernised the castle in some respects, including the provision of a piped water supply, traces of which can still be seen in the kitchen.

THE EARLS OF KENT AND THEIR TENANTS

On his father's death, Gilbert Talbot (1552–1616) became seventh earl of Shrewsbury, and the management of Goodrich

Castle and estate passed into the hands of a succession of tenants. The period of Talbot ownership finally came to an end in 1619, when Goodrich was claimed by the Crown as part payment for the debts of the dowager Countess Mary. The heiress of Goodrich, Gilbert and Mary's daughter Elizabeth (1582–1651), was married to Henry Grey, heir to the earldom of Kent, and it was to them that the castle passed just before the death of the dowager Countess in 1632. Meanwhile, the leasing of the castle to tenants continued.

In 1631–2 the castle buildings were repaired at the earl of Kent's expense. Some of the rooms were replastered, the glass was renewed and decayed stonework and timber were replaced. The works were supervised by a local attorney, Richard Tyler: as tenant of the earl he became constable of Goodrich, and lived in the castle with his family until 1644. In that year, he was to lose everything he had worked for, when Goodrich Castle suddenly became caught up in the struggle for control of Herefordshire and the Welsh Marches during the English Civil War which had broken out in 1642.

Left: A portrait of Gilbert Talbot, seventh earl of Shrewsbury, the last son of the Talbot family to own Goodrich Castle. From Memoirs of the Court of Queen Elizabeth, 1825, by Sarah, Countess of Essex, after a portrait by William Segar (d. 1633)

GOODRICH CASTLE IN THE CIVIL WAR

Though Goodrich Castle was apparently garrisoned by Parliamentarians in 1642, probably with the consent and assistance of Richard Tyler, it is principally associated with the Royalist cause. In the later months of 1643 the Royalists suffered a setback in failing to capture Gloucester, and urgently needed to check a northward Parliamentarian advance. In late 1643 or early 1644 a Royalist garrison was billeted at Goodrich Castle under the command of Henry Lingen (1612–62), who established his permanent headquarters there in September 1644. This development saw the imprisonment of Richard Tyler, who had prudently tried to sell livestock and other property before it was requisitioned. The Royalist takeover was evidently a violent one, with the 'burning and destroying' of the farm buildings on the site of Flanesford Priory, immediately below the castle.

In the following year there was intense fighting when the Royalist city of Hereford came under siege from a Parliamentarian army, and was only narrowly saved by a relieving army under the king's command. By the end of 1645 the city had been taken by the Parliamentarians and Goodrich Castle became the centre of Royalist activity in the area. Under the command of the newly knighted Sir Henry Lingen, a garrison numbering as many as 120 soldiers and 50 officers and gentlemen carried out raiding operations in the surrounding territory.

The local Parliamentarian commander was Colonel John Birch (1615–91), who first determined to hamper the Royalist operations by depriving the Goodrich garrison of its horses. A detachment of his men covertly entered the stables on the western side of Goodrich Castle on the night of 9–10 March 1646, stealing all the horses and torching the buildings (see page 25). But this action, though clearly a propaganda coup for Birch, had little lasting effect: the Parliamentarian army embarked on other operations elsewhere, allowing the Royalists to replace some of the lost horses and to resume their attacks around Goodrich.

THE SIEGE OF 1646

Some three months elapsed before Birch returned to Goodrich, this time determined to force Lingen and his garrison into submission. The vivid story of the negotiations and ensuing siege in June and July 1646 is told in great detail in a number of contemporary letters and in later accounts written by Colonel Birch and his secretary. The most significant outcome of this episode was the reduction of Goodrich Castle to ruin, a state in which it has remained ever since.

Birch returned to Goodrich on 1 June 1646, ordering new trenches to shelter his mortars under the walls. The Royalist commander Sir Henry Lingen refused to surrender and Birch found the castle too strong to break easily. To complement his cannon and mining operations, he ordered the casting in a local forge of a mortar able to fire a gunpowder-filled shell or grenadoe weighing 85kg (200 lb). This new mortar proved very effective and, like several other large artillery pieces of the period, was nicknamed Roaring Meg.

Birch concentrated his assault on the north-west tower, seen as a weak point in the castle's defences; mortar fire damaged the superstructure and its rock footings were undermined. This second operation was almost ruined when the Royalists dug a counter-mine underneath Birch's mine from the tower's basement. Birch, however, moved his mortar into close range at night and brought much of the tower down, burying the counter-mine. All was ready for the storming of the castle and on 31 July 1646 Lingen hauled down his colours, flying a white flag of surrender. Birch would not allow the Royalists to march out with their arms, regarding them as prisoners; they left the castle to a tune called 'Harry Lingen's Folly'.

After many years standing outside Hereford Museum, Roaring Meg, the only mortar to have survived from the Civil War, was returned to Goodrich Castle in 2003, and is now displayed at the north-east corner of the inner courtyard.

Above: *Statue in Weobley church, Herefordshire, showing Colonel John Birch, local commander of the Parliamentarian forces, who led the assault on Goodrich Castle in June 1646*

Below: *Roaring Meg, cast on the orders of Colonel Birch at Goodrich forge in June 1646, now stands in the courtyard at Goodrich Castle*

AFTER THE CIVIL WAR

The siege left the castle in a ruinous condition with 'noe whole room in it' according to Colonel Birch, though enough had survived for him to leave a garrison there and for Richard Tyler to return to his former home. For this reason, Parliament ordered that it be slighted, or rendered indefensible, by the removal of the battlements and damage to the main defences, and these works were completed in 1648. The castle remained the property of the dowager countess of Kent, whose family had supported Parliament; she therefore received £1,000 compensation for the demolition, which ironically was supervised by Richard Tyler himself. Goodrich Castle was now uninhabitable. Apart from a continuing use of the ditch as a cattle pound, it survived purely as a historical curiosity, its surrounding estate exploited for forestry, stone quarrying, ironworking and fishery.

The castle finally passed from the ownership of the earls (later dukes) of Kent in 1755, when it was sold to Admiral Thomas Griffin (1692–1771), with whose descendants it would remain until it came into the guardianship of HM Office of Works in 1920. From the 18th century until the present, the historical significance, architectural interest and scenic beauty have proved the most significant assets of Goodrich Castle, as it took on its latest role, that of a tourist attraction.

Top: A picturesque view of Goodrich Castle from across the Wye, by Theodore Henry Fielding, 1821
Above: *Watercolour by John Chessell Buckler of the gatehouse, south-east tower, keep and south-west tower, painted in 1827*

GOODRICH CASTLE AND THE WYE TOUR

Like nearby Tintern Abbey, Goodrich Castle attained new celebrity in the 18th and 19th centuries, as antiquarians and aesthetes were drawn to the Wye valley by its historic monuments and untamed scenery. Writers such as the Reverend William Gilpin, whose *Observations on the River Wye* was first published in 1782, popularised the concept of the Picturesque and inspired the growth of an early tourist industry, with organised itineraries, published advertisements for accommodation and guidebooks.

Lying some 6.5km (4 miles) downstream from Ross-on-Wye, Goodrich made an ideal first stopping point for travellers by boat. Visitors could either take in the distant view from the river or walk up a footpath from the ferry close to the present bridge, added in 1828. By the early 19th century the castle ruins were softened by ivy, wild roses and a famous ash tree in the courtyard. Visiting was a somewhat hazardous business, with ladders to enable the intrepid to reach the stairs in the keep, while local guides were on hand for historical information (and occasionally to sell historical souvenirs found in the ruins). From 1873 still greater numbers travelled along the valley by a new railway line, with a station close to the bridge: this finally closed in 1959.

Below: A photograph published in 1862 of the gatehouse from the barbican area, which was largely buried at this date

Bottom: The overgrown interior of the courtyard and remains of the solar block, photographed in about 1868

SIR SAMUEL RUSH MEYRICK AND GOODRICH COURT

From 1831 until 1949 the ruins of Goodrich Castle were overlooked by Goodrich Court, a spectacular mock castle designed by the architect Edward Blore for the scholar and collector Sir Samuel Rush Meyrick (1783–1848).

Searching for a suitable place to house and display his extensive collection of armour, Meyrick first visited Goodrich with his son in 1823, judging the ruined castle 'the very thing to suit us, so exactly that it seems to have been made on purpose'. Prevented from buying and restoring the actual castle, he finally built a new castellated house on the hill opposite. Externally the house was in 14th-century style, but the interior decoration was inspired by other countries in Europe and the Orient, as well as having more conventional neo-Gothic rooms. Meyrick created elaborate displays, including a 'south sea room' and a 'hastilude chamber' – a tableau of mounted knights jousting. With its pleasure gardens, armouries and furnishings, Goodrich Court became another popular attraction on the Wye Tour.

In 1871 the house was sold and much of the collection dispersed. Without its showpiece role, the building was too impractical to serve as a home, even after numerous alterations. After a final occupation in 1940 by an evacuated school (see opposite) it was eventually demolished in 1949, leaving only the gatehouse on the Ross–Monmouth road. The site of Goodrich Court is now a nature reserve.

Meyrick is buried beside his son in Goodrich churchyard. Part of his collection of armour is now in the Wallace Collection, London.

Above: Sir Samuel Rush Meyrick's neo-Gothic house, Goodrich Court, seen through the arch of the north range of Goodrich Castle in about 1840

Below left: A 16th-century suit of armour from Sir Samuel's collection, which he originally intended to house at Goodrich Castle

Below right: Sir Samuel's plan of the castle, showing his proposal to rebuild the ruins as a home and showplace for his collections. After his offers to buy the castle were refused, he created a similar set of rooms at Goodrich Court

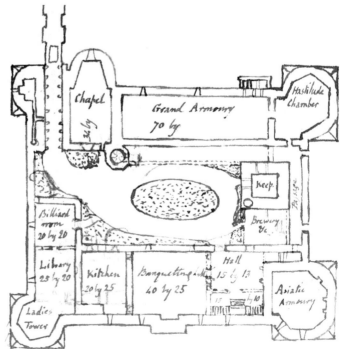

Memories of Goodrich

There was armour everywhere – one boy got stuck inside a Jacobean helmet and had to be rescued by the headmaster

Kenneth Kendall, former BBC newsreader, remembers being evacuated to Goodrich Court in the 1940s:

'Goodrich Court was in a marvellous position – Sir Samuel Meyrick knew what he was doing. It was across the valley from Goodrich Castle, above the River Wye. We often got into trouble with the castle curator for climbing on the walls.

'We had a wonderful view of the castle from the gardens of Goodrich Court. Felsted School moved there in 1940 because the Army wanted to take on the school buildings. In Essex, where the school was originally, there was the Battle of Britain – we were really in the thick of things. But at Goodrich, we felt miles away.

'The house was furnished with amazing furniture and paintings – a Van Dyck on the stairs, as well as two Canalettos and a Rembrandt. And there was armour everywhere. I remember one boy got stuck inside a Jacobean helmet and had to be rescued by the headmaster.

'We used to help the local farmers because all the workers had been called up: strawberry picking in the summer, and apples – Herefordshire is cider country. We were always hungry as there was strict rationing then. The bakers made wonderful bread and you'd eat the entire loaf just as it was. My dormitory was in the stables. Other boys stayed at Hill Court across the river. The scouts built a suspension bridge, so they could walk across. It didn't feel very safe!'

Below: The Great Hall of Goodrich Court in use as the school dining room by the Felsted School evacuees in the 1940s. The panelled walls were still hung with tapestries and armour

Above: The chapel photographed in the 1920s. The floor and ceiling were reinstated in 1957

Below: *The south-west tower scaffolded for conservation works in 1925, with the remains of the outer curtain wall in the foreground*

THE CASTLE AS AN ANCIENT MONUMENT

At the beginning of the 20th century the ruins of Goodrich Castle, though attractively covered in vegetation, were structurally in poor repair. In 1915 HM Office of Works entered into negotiations with the owner, Mrs Louisa Bosanquet, to take the site into state guardianship. These negotiations became more urgent in 1919 when large sections of the north-west tower and west curtain wall close to the great hall and vestibule collapsed into the ditch.

The Office of Works took responsibility for Goodrich in 1920 and over the following decades systematically cleared the vegetation from the site, consolidated the underlying stonework and rebuilt several areas of particularly decayed masonry with stones reused from elsewhere on the site. These works added greatly to the understanding of the castle's history, particularly the discovery in 1925 under the south-west tower of the foundations of an earlier tower. Unfortunately, other areas of original masonry that might have revealed more of the castle's earlier history were covered over and hidden by the new repairs.

As the 20th century progressed measures were also taken to improve access around the site, with a new staircase, floors and roofs in the gatehouse and chapel, a modern walkway along the east wall-walk and new stairs and bridges in the keep and south-east tower. Since 1984 the conservation and archaeological recording of the castle's fabric, together with its presentation to the public, have been the responsibility of English Heritage.